Quick Reads

The Red Boxing Gloves

Bicky and Miles want to learn to box but they always end up fighting. Maybe the red boxing gloves will make a difference.

Enjoy more *Quick Reads*

The Red Boxing Gloves
David Metzenthen
Illustrated by Meredith Plant

Wrestlefest Fever
James Roy
Illustrated by Damien Woods

Clever Sandwiches
Rowena Cory Lindquist
Illustrated by Kim Wilson

Race of Fear
Kathy Hoopmann
Illustrated by Stephen Axelsen

Quick Reads

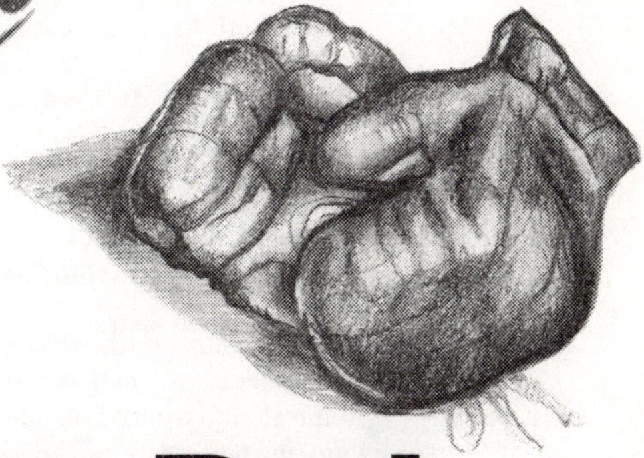

The Red Boxing Gloves

David Metzenthen

Illustrated by Meredith Plant

Word Weavers Press

D.M.—For Ella and Liam.

M.P.—For my kind and supportive friends and family

First published 2002 by Word Weavers Press Pty Ltd
PO Box 843 Bulimba, Queensland 4171, Australia

www.WordWeaversPress.com.au

1 3 5 7 9 10 8 6 4 2

Text copyright © David Metzenthen, 2002
Illustrations copyright © Meredith Plant, 2002

The moral right of the author and illustrator has been asserted.

All rights reserved. Without limiting the rights under copyright reserved above, no part of this publication may be reproduced, stored in or introduced into a retrieval system, or transmitted in any form or by any means (electronic, mechanical, photocopying, recording or otherwise), without the prior written permission of both the copyright owner and the above publisher of this book.

Typeset by Post Pre-press Group, Brisbane, Queensland
Printed in Australia by McPhersons Printing Group,
Maryborough, Victoria

National Library of Australia
Cataloguing-in-Publication data:

Metzenthen, David, 1958– .
The red boxing gloves.

For young readers.
ISBN 1 877073 07 5.

I. Plant, Meredith. II. Title. (Series: Quick reads).

A823.4

Chapter 1
OLD ENEMIES

Some kids like going to Mount Gary Youth and Fitness Club and some kids don't. Me? I love it. I go there every night it's open. I get there early and leave late. Terry, the guy who runs the joint, just laughs.

"Bicky," he says, shaking his head, "you're one hell of a hard case."

I am, too. My name might be (Vernon) "Bicky" Briscoe, but I'm hard as nails. I can do thirty-five push-ups no sweat, twenty-five on my knuckles. Some kids don't like boxing at all, but I do. That's all

I do at the club. Forget the ping pong table, forget the basketball ring. I hit the black punching bag till the sweat jumps off my nose, and then I keep on hitting. Everyone knows the black punching bag's my favourite because my dad gave it to the club. It's also the best one, so I use it all the time.

The black punching bag's got a picture of a boxer on it—he's like a ghost boxer now, he's been hit so many times he's almost faded away. When I first started to hit the black bag I used to pretend this boxer was my total enemy. I used to slam into him—*Whack! Whack!* Take that! *Slam! Bam!* Knock-out, man!

But now I've spent so much time with the old feller he's like my silent training partner. It took me a while to work out that the ghost boxer's on my side. I mean, he never hits back, so he must be! Now I send friendly thoughts to him like—"Watch this, ghost-guy"—*whack, smack, crack!* "Check this out"—*left hook, uppercut* . . . "You're outta here".

Tonight I'm the first one at the club, as usual. Except for Terry. Terry is skipping, his freckly brown arms sticking out of his T-shirt. Terry's a legend, my dad says. That's why he gave the black boxing bag to the club, to help Terry out.

   I drop my fifty cents into the tin, and go into the change room where the toilet always makes a sound like a choking monster, and the air always smells of old wet towels. I take off my tracky daks and windcheater then go back into the hall in my old black shirt with the sleeves cut off. I like this shirt, I like having no sleeves. It looks good, like I'm a stockman, or a brickie or something.

I pick up a skipping rope. It's no use killing yourself straight away, so I skip slowly, watching the open door to see who's going to turn up. Outside it's dark and the lights are on at the footy ground. I can see guys running laps around the boundary line, hand-balling as they go. Then a kid comes in the door.

And this kid is a kid I don't like.

His name's Miles Morgan and his old man is the big boss at the sand mine where my dad works. Miles is wearing a shiny red tracksuit with white stripes over the shoulders and brand-new Nike

runners. His brown hair's long and floppy at the front and neat and short at the back. Mine's the opposite, real short and blonde on top, longer at the back. I've got one ear pierced, too.

I see Miles drop a silver coin into the tin before he goes to the change room. We're roughly the same size. We always have been, even at primary school, even though we weren't in the same class. But now we're not at school together any more. I go to Mount Gary Secondary, but Miles goes to a big boarding school in Melbourne for rich kids. It's called McGregor Grammar. These days he only comes back to Mount Gary during the holidays.

I reckon Miles thinks he's great because his old man's got a red four-wheel drive and his family live in a five-storey house up on the hill—well, it *looks* like a five-storey house. I don't talk to Miles because he never talks to me. He's a snob. Bicky the Biscuit is a working-class dude and proud of it!

My old man says Miles's dad, Mr Morgan, wouldn't have a clue what it's like to drive an earthmover or use his hands, or do a day's hard yakka. My dad says Mr Morgan only thinks about dollars, and not about the blokes who work where it's dangerous. I bet Miles is just like his old man. I bet Miles is a real wuss who's never worked hard in his life—well, neither have I, but I will when I leave school.

Miles has decided to skip too. He's not as good as me. Skipping is cool if you can do it right. All boxers skip—world champions, Olympic gold medallists, all of them. I speed up three times faster to blow Miles away, then I take the pedal off the metal, slow down, and stop. So does Miles. We don't even nod at each other.

I get a pair of training gloves from the wooden box and so does Miles. Then I walk to the punching bags—and so does Miles, straight to the black bag my dad bought for the club. *What*! Well, I don't say anything. I just start to punch the brown bag that's as heavy and hard as clay.

Miles might only come here during school holidays, but everyone knows the black bag's the one I use. I mean, I don't own it, but Miles could've asked me if I wanted to start on it. I probably would've said "no". But he didn't ask and that's typical of him. He's just a spoilt rich kid who thinks *he* owns everything. So I pretend the brown bag is Miles Morgan and belt it so hard it swings on its chain like meat on a butcher's hook.

The first kid I see when I walk into the youth club is Vernon Briscoe. We used to go to school together, before my parents sent me to board at McGregor Grammar. Vernon's nickname is "Bicky". Everyone calls him Bicky—except me. I don't call him anything, because we never talk to each other. Still, if my name was *Vernon* I guess I'd want to be called Bicky, too. Not that my name is much better. In fact, it's probably worse. *Miles*! But I can live with it. I have to. My mum is pleased I'm the only Miles in the whole of my school. Man, I'm probably the only person called Miles in the whole world!

I put my fifty cents in the tin and go into the changing room. It stinks, but I don't really mind because it's a smell I remember clearly from the old days before I went to school in the city. It's a friendly smell, a Mount Gary smell. I take off my tracksuit, make sure my singlet hangs out over my shorts properly, and go back into the hall. I like this place. I always have. It's even better now, I notice, because there are more girls here.

I pick up a skipping rope and get started. I haven't skipped for months so I'm pretty hopeless. Bicky, of course, is letting me know how good he is. I can hear his skipping-rope whirring away like a fan, and when I glance over I see he's wearing a cut-off shirt like a lot of the guys around town wear. Bicky thinks he's a legend. I don't know what his problem is. Yes I do. He thinks just because his old man has a black V-8 ute and drives a brand-new Terex articulated tipper out at the mine, he's a tough guy. Well, my old man used to drive a fifty-tonne Euclid

when he was about twenty, but that doesn't make me feel that I have to cruise around as if I'm a commando in the S.A.S.

I drop the rope, say hello to Terry, who runs this place, then grab a pair of mitts and start punching the old black bag that

Bicky's dad gave to the club. It's the best bag, but I'd never tell Bicky that. I let go with a few big shots just to make sure my good friend Ver-*non* gets the point that I'm now just a bit bigger and stronger than he is. Okay, it's true I haven't been skipping much lately or hitting the bags, but I have been running laps and playing some hard footy—and I've been growing.

But really, I'm a fairly laid-back guy, and if Vernon-el-Bicky-el-Biscuito was just a bit cooler, I'd be prepared to have a truce. But he's not. I mean, I bumped into him one Saturday morning at Target and there he was, acting like a bouncer in the sock department. What's the point of that? Relax, I say! But he won't. And neither will I unless I get to see that the guy is worth it.

I slam the black punching bag left, right, left, to show Ver-*nooon* that if he wants to have a go at me he just might end up as one very badly crushed Biscuit.

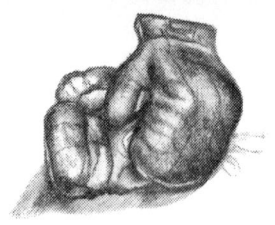

Chapter 2

COME OUT BOXING

Terry walks between the swinging bags. Miles and I stop punching. The noise of the club rushes in. Kids shout, basketballs bang, the ping pong ball clicks, an electric guitar screams out of the old cassette deck, and a couple of girls I know from school, Roslyn and Mischa are here. I look at them, but just for a couple of seconds or so.

Terry pushes his hand back through his crew cut. His hair's black with lots of grey in it. He's pretty old, about forty-three, but he's tough. He used to work at

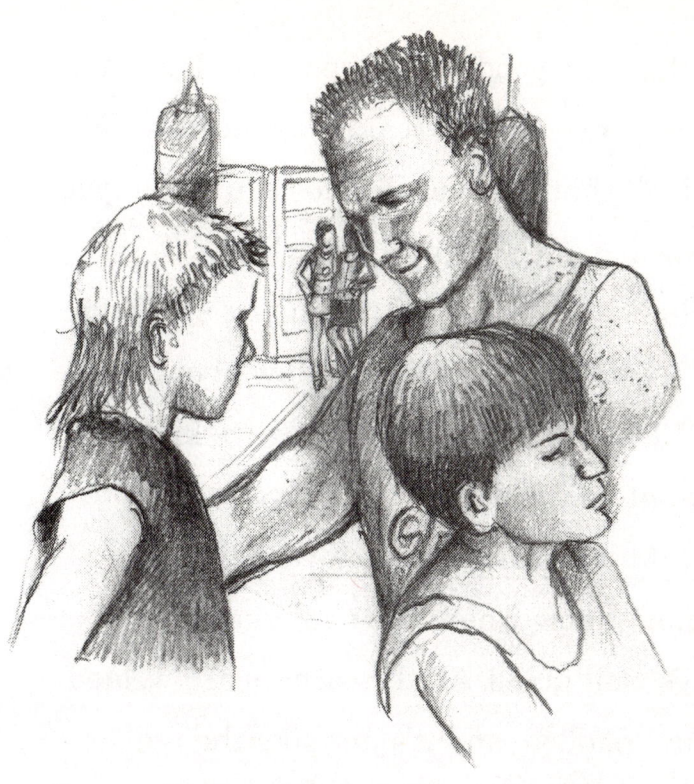

the sand mine, but now he runs the Mount Gary newsagency.

"You fellers want to spar a couple of rounds?" he asks Miles-Me-Say-Nothin'-To-Anyone, and yours truly. "Seeing as it's not that busy tonight?"

"Sure," I say, not looking at Miles,

"that'd be good." I like sparring. It's scary, but it gives you a real dangerous type of thrill that nothing else does. And it'll give me a chance to hit Miles, which is a chance that doesn't come along every day.

Terry looks at Miles. "How about it, Miles? Just easy stuff. You guys know what you're doing."

Miles nods, so we go over to the ring. I don't know where the ring came from, but it's well made. All the corners are welded and padded, and it's just like the real thing, only a bit smaller. I put on a red headguard, stick in my mouthguard, and pull on a pair of big old brown gloves. Miles does the same, then Terry does up the gloves for us and we climb in through the ropes.

"Take it easy, guys." Terry pushes us

back to a corner each. "This is a two-minute round. Keep your guard up and your chin down. Touch gloves, then come out boxing."

Terry asks me and Biscuit-boy if we want to spar a couple of rounds. I must admit I don't exactly feel like it, because I haven't done any boxing training since last holidays, but there's no way I'd admit I don't want to have a go. So I get into the ring, which my dad built one weekend with Terry, and prepare to face Ver-*ninny*, the lean, mean, fighting Teddy Bear Biscuit. He looks as if he thinks this is a world title fight. Over by the CD-player I see a couple of girls I remember from primary school.

They look across so I kind-of smile at them. Boy, they sure look different since I saw them last.

My dad did a good job building this ring. He and Terry designed it, cut and welded the steel, strung up the ropes, and bought the canvas. Dad said it was good to actually make something for a change, because he runs the sand mine now, and that's a job where he has to use his head rather than his hands. But he really likes his work, making sure everything runs smoothly and safely.

Terry helps me pull on the gloves. I'll admit that I'm a bit nervous about sparring. Boxing isn't like any other sport. Although you wear a helmet and mouthguard, you can still get hit and hurt. Rule number one, Milo-man, I tell myself, is: *Never drop your guard*. Rule number two, which is also very important, is: *Hit that Biscuit!*

"Take it easy, guys," says Terry, and steps back. "This is a two-minute round. Keep your guard up and your chin down. Touch gloves and come out boxing."

Don't worry, Terry, I'll do just that. And here comes the Biscuit, flying straight out of the barrel . . .

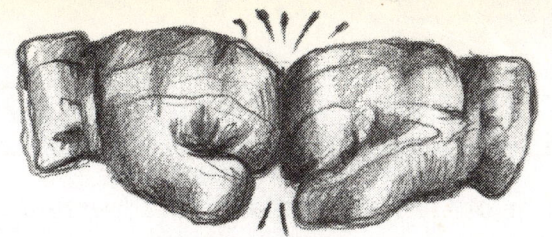

Chapter 3

CHAIN REACTION

Miles and I come out and put our gloves together, which is the same as shaking hands, which I could've done without, but it's a rule of boxing, so I obey it. Already I'm breathing quickly and my mouth feels fat because of my mouthguard. But I'm not scared, just nervous. I jab fast with my left glove and keep my right glove in front of my chin.

Miles ducks then jabs at me with his right. He's a southpaw, a left-hander, but who cares? I'll hit him no matter which hand he leads with. He jabs and misses;

quickly I step in and let go two punches, neither of them hard. One hits Miles on the cheek, pushing his head back. I go after him and hit him twice more, my fists firing out without me thinking.

Miles twists away then hits me in the stomach. I drop my guard and he gets me on the side of the head, but it doesn't hurt. I slide away watching him. Terry yells at me to keep my gloves up.

"And don't stand still!" he adds.

I let go a combination of punches. Some hit, some miss. Miles punches back, getting me on the front of my headguard. Then he hits me in the stomach again, but I see it coming, and it doesn't bother me at all. Now I go after him. *Thump! Smack! Whack!*

Suddenly a glove sizzles past my head

at a million kilometres an hour. Miles's face is red and his eyes look angry. He hits me in the ribs, I hit *him* in the ribs. Then I try a big left hook. It misses but puts him off-balance. So I try a right hook, which gets him on the side of his headguard.

Suddenly Terry jumps in between us and pushes us apart. He pokes a finger into my chest. "Take it easy, Bicky." *Poke.* "Or get out of the ring!" *Poke.*

I nod, push in my mouthguard, and try some fancy footwork. I come in really fast and low. I love speed. I always try to be the fastest. I let fly with lefts and rights. There's something cool about throwing lots of good quick punches. It's like I'm Sugar Ray Leonard or some champion guy like that. *Bang, bang, bang,* out they go one after the other, like bullets.

I don't mean to hit Miles hard, but sometimes I get a bit carried away, and this just might be one of those times. Miles comes after me, punching right, left, right. I sway back, step forward, jab with my left, and catch him smack on the cheek. He stumbles, his hands low. I could really thump him now, but I don't. I dance away, and take some big breaths, because Terry's watching me, and I must admit my arms are exhausted.

"Box on!" Terry yells. "Fifteen seconds to go!"

Miles pushes me onto the ropes, and suddenly his big brown gloves are coming at me from everywhere. I duck to get away, but punches are raining down on me one after the other. My head gets hit,

then one glove gets me right in the face. I want to yell at Miles to cut it out, that he's punching too hard. Instead I swing wildly with a couple of big hooks, then a straight right-hander. The hooks miss, but my straight right bops him on the nose and he staggers back.

Terry, like Superman, jumps between

us. "That's it! You guys are out of control! Get the gloves off!"

I'm breathing so hard my throat hurts. I can see Miles's nose is bleeding, which I'm happy about. I let my arms flop down to my sides. I must admit I'm not that worried about hitting him hard. In fact, inside I'm pleased. I don't care about punching someone who isn't one of my mates. Sparring with your friends is different. You don't want to hurt them. But *Miles*? The kid's a drop kick. Anyway, he started the rough stuff. I just finished it.

Terry unlaces my gloves, standing in front of me, looking at me with eyes the colour of bluestone rocks. He's not happy, I can see that. "You don't listen do you, Bicky? You weren't sparring, mate, you were just trying to hit. Sparring is about learning to box, not trying to hurt the other guy."

I don't care what Terry says. Miles had it coming to him. Instead of looking at Terry, I stare at the logo on the front of his shirt, advertising his Mount Gary newsagency.

Terry swings around. "You too, Miles. You're here to learn, not brawl."

Miles stands at the ropes, his face sweaty, a trickle of blood still coming from his nose. I take off my headguard and my face feels cool and good. I spit my mouthguard into my hand and stick it in my pocket.

Then Terry tells me to unlace Miles's gloves.

Unlace *his gloves*? Yeah, right. Give me a million bucks and I might. I shake my head. "No way," I say. "I ain't touchin' 'em."

Terry gets hold of my arm with strong fingers. He drags me one step forward, then smiles, only it's more like a snarl.

"You'll do it, *thanks*, Bicky. Now! I won't ask again."

Terry lets me loose. I've got no choice. So I do it, ripping at the laces, loosening the gloves, then I haul them off with two quick jerks and drop them on the ground. I don't say anything. I'm really angry. Terry should never have made me do that. And suddenly it's too much. I jump at Miles, he steps to one side, then jabs me with a punch.

"You stinkin'—" I let fly and we wrestle and hit until Terry drags us apart and yells at us.

"You guys wanna fight? You really wanna fight? Okay, this Thursday night, right here. Amateur rules. I'll referee—just us three. Okay?"

"Sure," I say, glaring at Miles-Me-No-Speak'a-The-Language, who just keeps on staring at me. "I'll kill him."

"You're kiddin' yourself!" Miles sniffs as if he needs to spit. "Ver-*non*," he adds.

I don't like my real name, and I don't like anyone using it. Especially someone called *Maaarles*. "You're gunna hit the deck," I say, "you're gunna get thumped, *Maaarles*. I'll splatter you, you cream puff."

Terry points at us both. "I'll even break out some new gloves. Nice red competition ones."

"Good," I tell him, "they won't show his blood so much."

I walk back to the change room. I never realised I hated Miles Morgan as much as I do. He'll get the message, though, when I flatten him. Actions speak louder than words around here, that's for sure.

Bicky comes in to start sparring, mean-faced in his headgear, gloves up. I jab and slide away, defence often being the best form of attack. I like to be a moving target. I mean, why stand still and let a Biscuit punch holes in you? So I dance, but already I can feel my legs are heavy. Bicky lands two punches, light ones, *bop*, *bop*. I tag him, *bang*, and move away.

I concentrate hard, watching Bicky's

eyes, but not only his eyes. I watch the whole of the Biscuit, so to speak, and I jab, keeping him away. Again he comes in. He's fast, I'll admit that. A couple of times he gets me, once pretty hard, but I throw a left and that lets him know Milo's still hanging in here. Then I slide forward, switching from defence to attack, and get him with two or three good shots. This the Biscuit does not like. The Biscuit likes to be the flashy fighter always going forward.

I can see he's angry now. *Thump*! He hits me with a punch that isn't the type you should throw when sparring. Now I'm mad, real mad, and when I get mad, I like to get even. I throw a jab, follow up with a right, and suddenly the sparring turns into boxing, and the boxing turns into fighting. Bicky and I stand toe to toe and throw punches as hard as we can, me trying to hurt him, him trying to hurt me, the boxing rule book gone right out the window. There are punches flying everywhere, some hitting, most missing.

Terry breaks us up, shoving us back with his elbows. "Take it easy or get out of the ring!" he warns Bicky. Then he gives me a dirty look. I nod. I know what he means: "*Spar, don't fight*". But when Bicky and I move in again for the last fifteen seconds of the round, I get the feeling it's going to be war—and I'm not wrong.

Bicky comes in punching hard, so I go flat-out. I don't care now. All I want to do is belt him, and I do, a couple of times; and boy, I have to admit, he belts me back. Then Terry shoves us away from each other, and that's that. I stand in my corner

wiping blood from my nose while Bicky stands in his, looking absolutely wild. I draw in big breaths; my nose feels about twice its normal size. But the last thing I'll do is show pain. No way. A blood nose is nothing.

Terry takes off the Biscuit's gloves. Then

he tells him to take off mine. This doesn't work so well because Bicky and I don't want to be anywhere near each other. In two seconds we're fighting again, going at it with bare fists until Terry jumps on us both.

"You guys wanna fight?" he yells.

I nod. I want to have a real go at Bicky. I want to flatten him. I'd like to do it right now. I'd like to knock him out—but Terry won't let us near each other again tonight. Instead he suggests that we fight on Thursday night, under amateur rules. Cool. I'll be here. And if Vernon the Chicken-Flavoured Biscuit has the guts to turn up—well, he'll wish he hadn't.

Chapter 4
READY TO RUMBLE

One night down, one full day left before the fight. And I'm ready to rumble. I train at home, skipping and shadow-boxing, and planning strategies. I feel a bit scared but not much. I noticed that Miles is bigger than me now, but I'm fitter and faster. And I'm meaner. On Thursday night Miles Zipper-Lips will wish he'd never stepped into the ring with Vernon the Junkyard Dog Biscuit.

I bet right now Miles is packing death. I bet he's never been in a real boxing match in his life. (Well, neither have I,

but I spar with Terry and he's really strong.)

    If Miles would've talked to me sometimes I wouldn't hate him so much. Once I asked him how his new school was, but he didn't answer me. That was in the Target sock department on a

Saturday morning. I was with my mum and he was with his. I wanted to belt him there and then, but our mothers kept talking, so I couldn't. Afterwards, Mum said she reckoned Miles was just shy. Shy! Pig's eye! Miles isn't shy. He just thinks he's Mr Hollywood because he owns about a thousand pairs of sports shoes and wears those little socks girl tennis players wear. Which is probably why he was in the Target sock department. To get some pink ones. Well, tomorrow night he'll find himself in the punch department, and it'll be one-way traffic from Mister Bicky's fists to Miles's million-dollar honker.

I shadow box, practising all my moves. Jab, right, left, uppercut, and away! Man, I'm like greased lightning. It's show time,

Miles! It's gunna be Black Thursday, boy! It'll be Miles-No-Smiles's worst nightmare! And there's no way he can get out of it, because Bicky the Blow Torch is on fire, and Miles Mini-Socks will burn. Believe me.

I don't have a skipping rope at home, so I go running instead. From the top of our hill I can see right over Mount Gary. I can even see the Biscuit's street. I bet old Bicky-boy will be down there training like a maniac. He'll be in his cut-off shirt, shadow-boxing, ducking and weaving, and hissing air out like a flat tyre. He's a legend in his own lunch box, that's for sure. But like a biscuit he's gunna be flattened tomorrow night good and proper, because Miles, the Big City Rolling Pin, will roll right over him.

At McGregor they call me "Bulldozer". On the footy field anyone I tackle stays tackled. Tomorrow night poor old Choc Chip is going to wish he was back in the biscuit packet—or back in the Target sock department with his mummy to protect him, because there'll be no one to save him in the boxing ring.

I'm not scared. Well, maybe I am a bit nervous, but it's good to be nervous, it keeps you on your toes—which is not where Bicky will be for too long. He'll be flat on his back wondering how a truck with a bull-bar managed to get through the front door of the Youth Club to flatten him.

I stop in the park at the top of the hill. It's a sunny day, and beyond the town I can see dry yellow paddocks and the conveyor belt at the mine. I throw a few practice punches. Nothing fancy. Just big, straight, laser-guided missiles that'll be right on target. Poor old Bicky, it's going to be out of that packet for him and into the fire, because from the word *GO* I'll be on the attack. He can dance and prance, skip and run, but in a boxing ring he can't hide. I'm going to work the angles, cut off his retreat, trap him in a corner, and in about three seconds we'll see how fast the Cookie crumbles.

It's nice up here in the park. The air is hot and clear. I feel good, but I'll feel better when this fight is over and I've won it. Bicky needs to be taught a lesson. He has to learn that there's more to being tough than cutting the sleeves off your shirt and having your ear pierced. He also has to learn that Miles Morgan is a real fighter. I'll beat the Bicky. It'll be back to the tin for him, back on the shelf. And if he wants to keep fighting—during school holidays, anyway—I'll be here, any where and any time. And that's a promise.

Chapter 5

FIGHT NIGHT

I get to the club at quarter past seven on Thursday night. No sign of Miles. He's probably trying to figure out which colour socks to wear, pink or yellow. I'm feeling nervous, but I'm ready to rock. Terry's here, he's got black jeans on and a white shirt and looks like a real referee—except that he's given the bow tie a miss.

"Get your gear on, Bicky," he says. "Miles ain't here yet."

I go into the change room and slowly take off my top layers. Underneath I've got on my cut-off denim shirt and clean black footy shorts. I get my mouthguard out and sit it in its box on the bench. My stomach's going round and I feel a bit spewy. Maybe I'm sick? Nah, I'm just nervy, that's all. Boxing's risky, sure, but that's why I do it. Out into the hall I go, all set.

Miles walks in. He doesn't look at me and I don't look at him. I shadow box and jog in front of the mirror. With every punch or jab I throw, my hair bounces and my arms feel powerful. I'm gunna hurt the guy, for sure. I'm ready to go. The Hard-Case Working-Class Biscuit from the Wrong Side of the Tracks is ready to flatten Milo the Sock and Shoe Collector from Snob Towers.

Miles comes out of the change room. He's a couple of centimetres taller than

me and perhaps a couple of kilos heavier, but I'm not scared. I beat him Tuesday night and I'll beat him again tonight. Terry walks across the hall, his shoes scuffing lightly on the old wooden floor.

"Over here, fellers," he gestures. "Good to see you both."

We walk over. I make sure to put my shoulders back and stick my chest out.

"Okay," says Terry, "you guys go out the back and wait till I call you. Then we'll glove up and get into it, all right? I've just gotta find some tape, set the time clock, fill the water bottles and do some other stuff."

Miles and I both nod. We go back into the change room to wait. I stand and Miles sits. Then after a while I sit for a minute. Then I get up again. Man, what is going on here? I walk around, but I don't want to show too much, so I just move my hands, not even shadow boxing really. Come on, Terry, let's get this thing started! I mean, let's get it on! Why are we in here together?

Miles says nothing (how unusual), so I

say nothing too. He stands so I sit, to save energy. I sit there looking at the toes of my runners, smelling the dirty old towel smell, listening to the noisy toilet. Miles keeps his back to me. Good. I hope he's saying goodbye to his fat old nose because in about five minutes he's going to need a new one.

Terry comes in through the door. "There's a bit of a problem, boys," he says. "The new gloves aren't in the car. I must've left 'em at home in the garage. Wait right here—I'll be back in ten minutes."

Oh, great. Ten minutes of smelly silence with Miles Morgan the Small Sock and Super Shoe Expert. Boy, can you imagine 'Marvellous' Marvin Hagler and Tommy 'Motor City' Hearns sitting down for ten minutes together before a big fight? No way.

I walk into the Youth Club and say hello to Terry. I see Bicky-el-Biscuito over by the ring jogging slowly on the spot. Hopefully he'll tire himself out.

"Go and get ready, Miles," Terry says to me. "Then come on out. How ya feeling?"

"Good," I say, and head off into the change room. I take off my tracksuit, make sure my singlet's hanging right, take a good deep breath, and head back out into the club. Terry calls Bicky and me over, tells us that just about everything's set, and to go and wait out the back. So Bicky and I go back to the change room. I start to get the feeling of what it must be like for real boxers just before they go into the ring. Except that real boxers don't have to sit in the same place as their opponents. I mean, that could lead to trouble. Like, the main event might happen in the change room and no one would even get to see it.

The last place I want to be is in this stinking old room with the world's toughest Biscuit, but I do what I'm told, and take a seat. Even my hands feel nervous and my breathing feels shallow and quick. No way I'm going to let *Vernon* see I've got the shakes, so I shake my wrists to keep them loose. Then Terry comes in and tells us he has left the gloves at home. Oh, wonderful.

"Wait here," he says. "I'll be back in ten minutes."

So Bicky and I wait, the toilet keeping us company with its usual gurgling and gargling. Now I roll my shoulders and nod my head to keep myself loose. Then I stand up, do a few calf stretches, touch my toes, then stretch my triceps and biceps. I'm tempted to practise a few punches, but I don't. I jog on the spot, stop, then sit down again. Man, time passes slowly when you've only got a Tic-Toc Biscuit for company. I stand up again, but I can't think of anything more to do, so I sit down again. This is *ridiculous*!

Terry disappears. I listen to his footsteps leave the hall then hear his car start. Silence. It goes on and on, except for the toilet. I don't like silence much. If I was with one of my mates we'd be talking and mucking around, chucking stuff, or something. Miles gives me a look. I give him a look, but I can't put too much toughness into it because that would only be—well, stupid. I mean, it feels like we've been in here for about three hours,

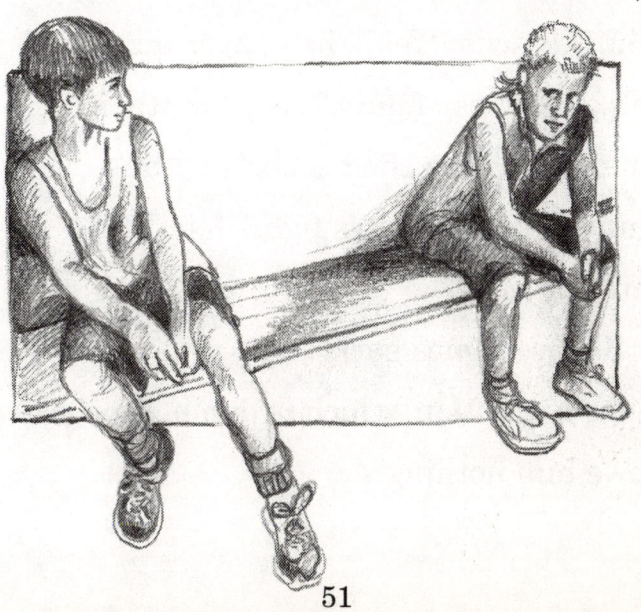

so it'd be a bit dumb to start putting on the hard face now.

"Who's your favourite boxer?" Miles asks me out of the blue.

For a few seconds I don't say anything. I know I should tell him to rack off, but I don't really feel like it. To tell the truth I'm kind of ready to talk, to break the tension.

"Kostya Tszu," I say. "The Russian guy from Sydney. Undisputed triple world champion. He's fantastic."

Miles nods. "Yeah, he's super quick and he's got heaps of guts." He grins, then puts one foot on the bench. "And he's funny. Plus he always fights fair. He's a hero, all right."

Silence comes back. I feel as if I owe Miles a question, which is dumb, because I owe him nothing.

"What's it like livin' in Melbourne?" I ask.

Miles isn't pacing around like a boxer about to fight, but sitting still, looking at his shoes, which aren't as new as I thought. He's got footy socks on too, which is a surprise.

"It's all right," he says, looking down the change room at me. "Sometimes I wish I was back here, though. At my school someone's always watching you, telling you what to do, or where to go. I mean, I live at the place, so someone's always got an eye on you. It's not that bad. I've got my own room and stuff. But you can't sleep in, or do any of that kind of thing."

Man, I would *not* like that. I couldn't stand being around teachers all the time,

including the weekends! Suddenly I remember something else about Miles's school—there are *no girls*! None. Zip. Zilch. Zero.

"You oughta come back to Mount Gary," I say. "There are babes here. Did you see those two girls who were here on Tuesday night? Roslyn and Mischa? They used to go to Mount Gary State. Man, they've put on a bit of . . . well, they've added a few curves."

Miles laughs. It surprises me. Like, I didn't think he would know how to laugh. Or maybe he would pay someone to do it for him.

"Yeah, I saw them," he says. "I remember them from last year. If they're here next Tuesday night I'd like to say hello and stuff."

"Sure," I say. "Hey, I ran into them at the milkbar yesterday and they, um, asked about you." Which they did— although I wasn't all that cool about Miles. I—well, I kind of canned him behind his back.

Miles looks surprised. He pushes his fringe back. "They asked about me? Hey. All right." He looks pleased. "You know, we do these dancing classes with this all-girls' school in town, and on the second night I fell over and fractured my wrist. A first in the history of the school."

I have to laugh at that. I mean, if that had happened to me, I wouldn't have had the guts to tell anyone. Maybe Miles isn't as hopeless as I thought. He seems to be—well, not so stuck up.

"That last punch you got me with on Tuesday," he adds, holding up his right hand. "Geez, I didn't even see it coming."

I try not to look too smart about it. It was a good shot, but lucky as well. "Yeah, I just got lucky," I say. "I mean, you were all over me so it was like a desperate move." I stand up, go to the door, and look out into the empty hall. The punching bags are still. No sign of Terry. "C'mon, I'll show you on the bag."

So we go across to the black bag, and as I'm showing Miles the combination and the footwork of the shot, Terry turns up. He hasn't got the gloves. By now I've almost forgotten about the fight, and when I do remember it, I'm not so hot for it any more. To tell the truth, I wouldn't mind giving it the flick. What's the use of fighting when you're not angry any more with the person you're supposed to be fighting? Or there's no trophy or medal to win or anything?

"I've lost the gloves," Terry says, and shows us his empty hands. "I must've driven off with 'em on the car roof or something." He pats the black punching bag as if it was a dog. "Look, maybe we'll just train a bit tonight, and forget the fight. Those big brown gloves are getting on a bit. I don't want anyone getting cuts or grazes. What d'you reckon?"

There's silence again. I can't even hear the toilet in the change room.

"Suits me," I say. "Of course, I would've won by a mile."

"Oh, yeah?" says Miles. "You couldn't beat an egg."

Terry holds up his hands. It's his way of telling people to keep quiet. "All right, this is what we'll do. We'll jog back to my place and see if we can find the gloves on the road. Then perhaps you blokes can pull 'em on next Thursday night."

"I'll be back at school," says Miles.

"You can spar with the girls at dancing classes, then," I say.

Miles pushes me, but he's only joking. I push him back, which makes us even.

"On that note," says Terry, laughing like he's got a cough, "I think we'll call it a draw. Come on, guys, help me lock up, and we'll go out and do a little bit of roadwork."

So outside we go, and the first thing that happens is we see Roslyn and Mischa. I remember I was telling them about the fight at the milkbar.

"Who won?" Mischa calls out from over the road, her blonde hair swishing around.

"It was a draw," Terry calls back.

"Can I have your phone number, Miles?" Roslyn yells.

I laugh and so do Terry and Miles. We stop.

"Of course you can!" I yell back. "Come 'n' get it!"

The girls race across the road laughing. Miles looks embarrassed, but Terry seems to be enjoying himself.

"Here you go, Miles," says Terry, and takes out a pen and notebook from his top pocket. "A good referee and a good newsagent always carries a pen and paper. Start writing."

Chapter 6

WHO WON?

When I get home my dad's waiting for me. The night footy's on TV and he's reading *Street Machine*. He puts it down.

"How'd the fight go, mate?" His black moustache twitches at the corners of his mouth. "Where's the world title belt?"

"We didn't fight," I say, sitting on the floor next to my red bag. "Terry lost the new gloves. We had to go and look for 'em, but we couldn't find 'em."

My dad opens up the magazine again. He loves the done-up old Holdens. "Well, old Terry'd be a goose, then," he says, then

looks at me across the pages. "What's that Morgan kid like, anyway? I was talkin' to his old man today. He was tellin' me how he used to drive the big earth movers in the mines, over there in the west."

I think about Miles and how things went at the club tonight. "Yeah, he seems okay," I say carefully. Suddenly I decide that Miles Morgan is like the faded ghost boxer on the black punching bag; he doesn't say much, he's a bit of a mystery, but he's not a bad guy. In fact, I guess he's a pretty good guy . . . once you get to know him. "Yeah, he seems all right once ya talk to him. Yeah, he seems okay."

My dad opens the door for me when I get home from the club.

"You're still alive, mate," he says. "How's young Bicky? You didn't kill him, I hope."

I put my bag down. Below us the streets of Mount Gary are lit up by rows of streetlights, but there's no one around, and hardly any cars on the road.

"We didn't fight," I say. "Terry lost the new gloves we were going to use, and in the end we just went out and did some roadwork. It was okay."

"Geez," my dad says. "Lost the gloves? Well, these things happen. How do you get on with that Bicky Briscoe? Is he a good kid?"

I look down to the part of the town where Bicky's house is.

"Yeah, he seems okay," I say. "He's not like I thought he was. He's pretty funny, actually."

My dad follows me inside and shuts the door. "I was talking to his dad today. He's all right too—he's fair dinkum and he knows how to work. Hey, Miles—"

"Yeah?" I slide my bag towards the door of my room. It doesn't make it.

My dad moves his shoulders around as if he's loosening up for something. Oh no, not more boxing!

"If you really don't like it down in the city," he says, "you'll tell me, won't you? If you reckon you'd do as well at school back here, I could talk to Mum."

Now there's something to think about.

"Thanks, I'll think about it," I say, and I will, but not right now, because I've got a phone call to make.

I grab the phone and go into my room. Out of my window is another view of Mount Gary. It's a small place, but a good place, I reckon—although I don't mind living in the city, either. I guess I'll stay there for a while. After all, I've got mates in *two* places, and that's got to be a bonus. I dial Roslyn's number, and wait to see what might happen.

"Hello," a voice says. "Roslyn Callendar speaking. Who is it, please?"

"It's Miles Morgan." I say. "From the, ah, Youth Club. You know, tonight."

"Oh, *hi*," Roslyn says. "Yes, you're Bicky's friend, aren't you? He's a funny kid, isn't he? I'm glad you didn't have the fight, aren't you?"

"Yeah," I say, and I come up with the perfect way to answer all those questions with just three words. "You're right there."

David Metzenthen

David lives in Melbourne, is married and has two children. He has been writing stories for young people for over fifteen years and although he is no longer young himself, he hopes his stories will be enjoyed by those who are. David has done some boxing, but was never, ever going to be a boxing champion.

Meredith Plant

Meredith has always wanted to be an artist. At school she was always in trouble for drawing in her books rather than doing her work. Once she was accidentally punched in the nose and it really, really hurt. Since then she has realised it is better and less painful to talk and listen to people. It's even better to draw them. Meredith lives on Tamborine Mountain with her family.